WILDFLOWERS
of COLORADO

Photography and Words
by John Fielder

Colorado Littlebooks

Westcliffe Publishers, Inc., Englewood, Colorado

First frontispiece: Daisies proliferate along the Stony Pass Road,
Rio Grande National Forest
Second frontispiece: The first week in June brings great fields of dandelions,
Wet Mountain Valley
Third frontispiece: Paintbrush, Columbine, and Larkspur cover
the slopes of the Mosquito Range
Opposite: Paintbrush and Showy daisies drink from Lake Creek,
Sawatch Range

International Standard Book Number: 1-56579-085-5
Library of Congress Catalog Number: 94-61068
Copyright John Fielder, 1994. All rights reserved.
Published by Westcliffe Publishers, Inc.
P.O. Box 1261, Englewood, Colorado 80150-1261
Publisher, John Fielder; Creative Director, Leslie Gerarden
Printed in Hong Kong by Palace Press International

For more information about other fine books and calendars from
Westcliffe Publishers, please call your local bookstore,
contact us at 1-800-523-3692, or write for our free color catalog.

PREFACE

Colorado is a great place to be if one enjoys colors. I don't mean yellow cabs and neon signs, I mean the colors that nature provides through the plants that grow on our planet Earth. Every plant has a flower, and each flower has a particular color — or even several. The range of colors one finds in wildflowers seems almost infinite.

To the eye of the nature photographer, this incredible variety of hues presents a wealth of subject matter. One of the great joys for me in traveling the state to photograph the landscape has been discovering this vast array of beauty.

This book is not intended as a guide to wildflowers; there are numerous books that have been published for that purpose, including a two-volume set published by Westcliffe. This book is merely for the sake of spreading a little joy through the medium of color photography. It is one man's visual interpretation of the Colorado landscape, with the purpose of celebrating the spectacle of wildflowers with which this state is blessed.

All of the wildflowers that grow in Colorado are not represented in this small book. To the contrary, I am woefully short of that goal and likely couldn't even accomplish that in a larger format book. However, most of the state's popular and commonly recognized wildflowers are pictured here: Indian paintbrush, Parry primrose, bluebells,

lupines, larkspur, daisies, and dandelions, as well as the Colorado columbine, the state flower.

I have chosen thirty-four of my favorite wildflower images, photographs I have made over the past twenty years. These images represent scenes that best showcase wildflowers in their natural environment. My intention was to create a feeling of "place," with the viewer envisioning him or herself in the scene.

Wildflowers can be found along any Colorado highway, backcountry byway, or hiking trail. But to me, the most fascinating flowers are those of the alpine domains. In the high country there is a continuing parade of color as flowers bloom throughout the growing season, from the first avalanche lilies pushing up in spring to the last blossoms of sneezeweed bent over in a wet October snow. The best years for wildflowers, I have found, are in years of heavy winter snows and consistent summer rains.

Flowers growing at the very highest elevations hold a particular appeal for me. The tundra is a harsh, windswept environment where only the hardiest of plants can grow. There, usually in July after the snows have melted, tiny flowers begin to bloom among the dense, spongy matting of grasses and mosses. If you have never seen the iridescent blues of forget-me-nots, the whites and pale violets

Orange sneezeweed loses this year's life to early snows, San Juan Mountains

of phlox, or the magenta of alpine clover, a hike above timberline is a wonderful experience.

Appreciating the beauty of wilderness is one of the most satisfying ways to enrich our lives. For me, a retreat into nature is a necessity. When I go to the mountains, whether to photograph or not, I add to the experience by being vigilant, by closely observing the colors, shapes, smells, sounds, and changes in light. These all influence and stimulate the senses. I hope that this book, its photographs and words, helps to stimulate the senses of those who view it, and in doing so helps foster an appreciation for the joys of nature, whether it be found in a single blossom or in a mountain meadow filled with wildflowers.

— John Fielder
Englewood, Colorado

Other fine books by John Fielder:

A Colorado Winter (1998)
Along Colorado's Continental Divide Trail (1997)
Photographing the Landscape: The Art of Seeing (1996)
Cooking with Colorado's Greatest Chefs (1995)
Explore Colorado (1995)
Rocky Mountain National Park: A 100 Year Perspective (1995)
A Colorado Autumn (1994)
The Complete Guide to Colorado's Wilderness Areas (1994)
A Colorado Kind of Christmas (1993)
To Walk in Wilderness: A Colorado Rocky Mountain Journal (1993)
Colorado, Rivers of the Rockies (1993)
Along the Colorado Trail (1992)
Colorado's Canyon Country: A Guide to Hiking & Floating BLM Wildlands (1992)
Colorado, Lost Places and Forgotten Words (1989)
Colorado Reflections Littlebook (1994)
Colorado Waterfalls Littlebook (1994)
Colorado Wildflowers Littlebook (1994)

Also look for John Fielder's Colorado wall and engagement calendars.

John Fielder's images are also available as limited edition prints and stock photography. For more information contact Westcliffe Publishers at 1-800-523-3692.

Showy daisies drink from an afternoon shower, White River National Forest

Beneath the gaze of distant peaks
Our yellows shine for so few weeks
It's such a shame our brilliance here
Can't be 'round throughout the year

False lupine below West Spanish Peak,
Culebra Range

Up close our petals seem to smile
Above the sea beyond a mile
Our scrawny stems they seem to be
About as tall as any tree

Nuttall sunflowers in the Wet
Mountain Valley

This flower's beauty is so great
It is the choice within our state
When friends they ask to know what's fine
I often say "the columbine"

Yellow columbine and Mountain bluebell,
Sawatch Range

It's name so strange I can't guess why
Unless you have the nerve to try
To put your nose so very close
And breathe inside a heavy dose

Orange sneezeweed, Maroon Bells-
Snowmass Wilderness

With all the days of summer rain
We try to steal the forest floor
But when the wet begins to wane
Our roots they say they'll spread no more

Arnica, White River National Forest

Bright yellow do its flowers boast
In spring you tend to see the most
Its name implies it lives for snow
But underneath it will not grow

Avalanche lilies,
Maroon Bells-Snowmass Wilderness

At home our lawns we try to spray
To keep these flowers far away
But when they grow across the hills
They are the last thing we would kill

Dandelions below Lizard Head Peak,
San Miguel Mountains

Across the valley they do spread
Without regard for where they tread
They'd best watch out for Farmer Fred
He'll hitch the plow and they'll be dead

Nuttall sunflowers below the Sangre de
Cristo Mountains

It is too late for I do fear
It's not the time to try to grow
For don't they see that it's quite clear
That Winter's here with all its snow

Yellow paintbrush,
Maroon Bells-Snowmass Wilderness

They paint pastels across great fields
To nothing do they think to yield
And pink and green do complement
So when they spread we won't lament

Blue-eyed grass, South Park

This tree it left us long ago
Who'd take its place we did not know
So now we try to fill that space
With colors for a special place

Columbine, Paintbrush, and Senecio,
Mosquito Range

I do not think they will grow wild
They take a climate much more mild
It must have taken human hands
To bring this flower to our land

Poppies, along the Yampa River

Where else would be a better place
To park yourself and slow the pace
Perhaps to sit and check the map
Or better yet to take a nap

Parry primrose, along Norris Creek,
Mt. Zirkel Wilderness

A weed we're called we do protest
For certainly we are the best
When color is of prime import
We are unique to any sort

Fireweed, along Schofield Pass, near
Crested Butte

A setting sun doest make the earth
Turn color so to up its worth
For setting suns illuminate
The plants that make our earth so great

Crimson saxifrage, Yampa River Valley

Without the sun the shade besets
A special hue on all that's wet
Without the sun they will not fade
All flowers gain another shade

Indian paintbrush, Sangre de Cristo
Mountains

Who'd believe there was no florist
To cultivate what's here before us
No I paid for neither flower
Twas all the work of nature's power

Wild iris, Wet Mountain Valley

They drink from rain and summer dew
And tend to grow near water, too
Without such moisture there would be
No flowers there for us to see

Mountain bluebell, Indian paintbrush,
Arnica, and Columbine

A streak of light pervades the trees
And look at what we barely see
A trio standing tall and proud
To prove that three is not a crowd

Colorado columbine, White River
National Forest

The rocks they try so hard to keep
The plants from going very deep
But here the smallest bit of earth
Is just enough to prove their worth

Colorado columbine,
Maroon Bells-Snowmass Wilderness

Summer storms they try to make
The rain each day that flowers take
So when we visit their domain
Their brilliant color will not wane

Elephant head, Raggeds Wilderness

A garden here we come across
I must admit I'm at a loss
Just how could nature make this place
The gardener vanished — he left no trace!

Elephant head, Paintbrush, Senecio, and
others, along the Howard Fork of the San
Miguel River, San Juan Mountains

The sun when shining from behind
Lights up the world so we will find
New things we never saw before
And make us feel we once were poor

Fireweed and Senecio, along the
Hagerman Pass Road

Perceptive eyes they see great things
To lesser things do others cling
Perceptive eyes eschew great haste
So look ahead and slow your pace

Forget-Me-Not and Clover at 13,000 feet
above sea level, Mosquito Range

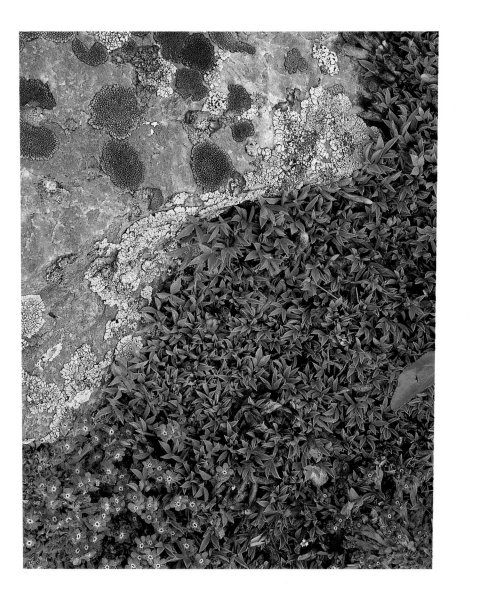

We lay beneath great trees that may
Protect us each throughout the day
For we provide them a great view
We think they know that we are due

Paintbrush and Lousewort, Arapaho
National Forest

Great things do happen here on high
The sun, the rain they both do vie
To be the biggest reason why
These flowers here will never die

Paintbrush, Columbine, Arnica, and
Larkspur, above the town of Telluride